CORNERSTONES OF FREEDOM™

WORLD WAR II

BY R. CONRAD STEIN

CHILDREN'S PRESS®
An Imprint of Scholastic Inc.
New York Toronto London Auckland Sydney
Mexico City New Delhi Hong Kong
Danbury, Connecticut

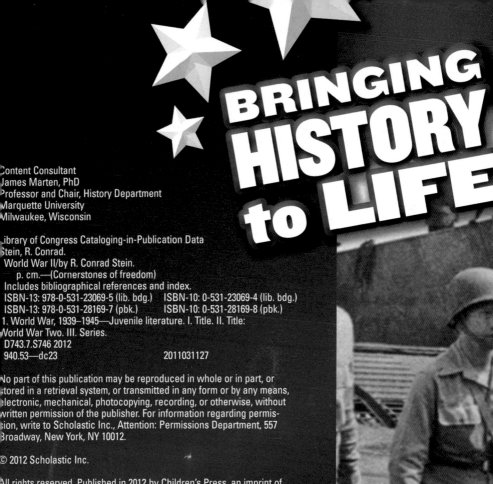

BRINGING HISTORY to LIFE

Content Consultant
James Marten, PhD
Professor and Chair, History Department
Marquette University
Milwaukee, Wisconsin

Library of Congress Cataloging-in-Publication Data
Stein, R. Conrad.
  World War II/by R. Conrad Stein.
    p. cm.—(Cornerstones of freedom)
  Includes bibliographical references and index.
  ISBN-13: 978-0-531-23069-5 (lib. bdg.)   ISBN-10: 0-531-23069-4 (lib. bdg.)
  ISBN-13: 978-0-531-28169-7 (pbk.)   ISBN-10: 0-531-28169-8 (pbk.)
  1. World War, 1939–1945—Juvenile literature. I. Title. II. Title:
World War Two. III. Series.
  D743.7.S746 2012
  940.53—dc23   2011031127

  2 3 4 5 6 7 8 9 10 R 21 20 19 18 17 16 15 14 13 12

Photographs © 2012: age fotostock/DEA Picture Library: 11; Alamy Images:
back cover (Lordprice Collection), 36 (Photos 12); AP Images: 24 (U.S.
Official Photo), 55 (Werner Kreusch), 4 top, 6, 7, 12, 16, 18, 20, 22, 26, 28,
31, 35, 44, 49, 58; Getty Images: 54 (Carl Mydans/Time & Life Pictures),
cover (FPG), 5 top, 15 (GAB Archive/Redferns), 47 (Keystone/Hulton
Archive); Library of Congress: 8 (Acme), 37, 56 bottom (Maurice Constant);
National Archives and Records Administration: 21, 57 (ARC 540153), 25
Army Signal Corps Collection), 2, 3, 45 (Department of the Army/ARC
531424), 27 (Department of the Army/ARC 594425), 42 (Department of the
Navy/80-G-17054), 14 (Department of the Navy/ARC 295977), 38 (Department
of the Navy/ARC 520621), 46 (Department of Transportation/U.S. Coast
Guard/ARC 513219), 40 (Office for Emergency Management/Office of War/
ARC 535553), 5 bottom, 30 (Office of War Information/ARC 535567), 32 (War
Relocation Authority/ARC 537040), 34 (Women's Bureau/ARC 522892);
Shutterstock, Inc./Sam DCruz: 51; Superstock, Inc.: 41 (Everett Collection),
0 (Image Asset Management Ltd.), 23 (Prisma), 50 (USAF/Image Asset
Management Ltd.), 13, 56 top; US Army/Center of Military History/SC196716;

Did you know that studying history can be fun?

BRING HISTORY TO LIFE by becoming a history investigator. Examine the evidence (primary and secondary source materials); cross-examine the people and witnesses. Take a look at what was happening at the time—but be careful! What happened years ago might suddenly become incredibly interesting and change the way you think!

Contents

4

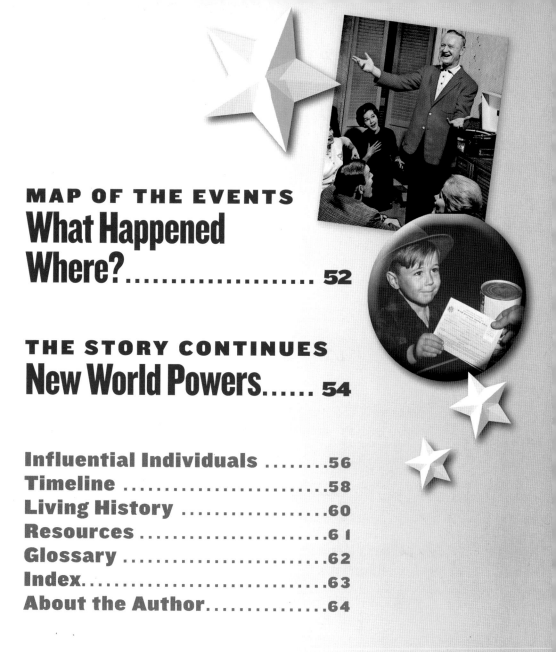

The Last War?

Adolf Hitler's talent for delivering speeches helped him gain control of Germany.

The battlefields of Europe fell silent when World War I ended in November 1918. The war was horrible. **Casualties** numbered in the millions. Many people believed that human beings had finally learned a lesson and would never wage war again. For a brief time, World War I was called "the war to end all wars."

Germany was the main loser in World War I. Its economy and military were both destroyed. A war veteran named Adolf Hitler used this depression to gain power in Germany. He claimed to be a German patriot and the nation's savior. Hitler was a fiery speaker. He blamed the Communists and the Jews for Germany's problems. He knew that placing the blame on them would cause Germans to rally together under his leadership. Hitler led a political party called the Nazis. He rose to become the leader of Germany in 1933.

On the other side of the world, Japan carved out what it hoped would be a huge empire. In 1931, Japanese armies invaded Chinese territory on the Asian mainland. An undeclared war broke out between Japan and China in 1937. Large portions of China soon fell under Japanese control. People had not learned their lesson from World War I after all. An even larger war was on the horizon.

Japan established control over a great deal of Chinese territory after the invasion of 1931.

SIX YEARS AND ONE DAY.

CHAPTER 1

THE BEGINNING

German troops caused severe damage to parts of Poland during the invasion.

GERMAN TROOPS INVADED THE neighboring country of Poland on September 1, 1939. Great Britain and France were allies of Poland. They had promised to defend Poland against a German attack. But Hitler refused to let this stop his plans. He was more concerned about the Soviet Union. Before invading Poland, the Germans negotiated a pact with the Soviets. The two countries secretly agreed to split Poland between them. Great Britain and France declared war on Germany two days after the invasion. Historians regard the 1939 attack on Poland as the start of World War II. World War I, "the war to end all wars," had concluded just 21 years earlier.

German troops entered Paris, France, on June 14, 1940.

Lightning War

German troops in tanks and aircraft raced across Poland and forced the country to surrender in three weeks. The Germans used a style of fighting called **blitzkrieg**, or lightning war. Hitler's armies advanced at breathtaking speed compared to the slow **infantry** movements of World War I. After taking over Poland, Germany set its sights on France. The French were quickly overpowered. They surrendered in June 1940. Soon after, Italy joined Germany in a military alliance. Italy was led by a **dictator** named Benito Mussolini. Mussolini dreamed of restoring his nation's past power and might. In September 1940, Germany, Italy, and Japan signed a pact together. This officially established them as the Axis powers.

Despite their agreement over Poland, Germany targeted the Soviet Union on June 22, 1941. Conquering the Soviets had been part of Hitler's plan from the beginning. Blitzkrieg strategies succeeded again as German forces pushed deep into Soviet territory. But the Soviets were able to stop the Germans in front of the capital city of Moscow. The Battle of Moscow was the first major setback for Germany. The Soviets became part of the Allied forces after the German invasion.

The Soviet forces used powerful artillery to help repel German troops during the Battle of Moscow.

During the bombings, the subway tunnels in London became so crowded with people seeking shelter that many had to sleep on the train tracks.

Britain Stands Alone

German aircraft began bombing Great Britain in July 1940. The bombs rained down on crowded cities such as London. Thousands of civilians died. Londoners often took shelter in their city's subway system during the attacks. A Londoner named Rosemary Black later wrote about her experience taking shelter in a subway: "Seeing every corridor and platform in every station all along the line crowded with people huddled three deep, I was too appalled for words. The misery of that wretched mass . . . the heat and smell, the dirt, the endless crying of the poor babies. . . . "

War Comes to America

December 7, 1941, began as a peaceful Sunday at the U.S. naval base in Pearl Harbor, Hawaii. But the soldiers and sailors heard a distant buzzing of aircraft at 7:55 a.m. Suddenly, a bomb exploded over Ford Island in the middle of the harbor. Japanese planes screamed from the sky. One plane machine-gunned the deck of the battleship USS *Nevada* just as men raised the U.S. flag and a marine band played "The Star Spangled Banner."

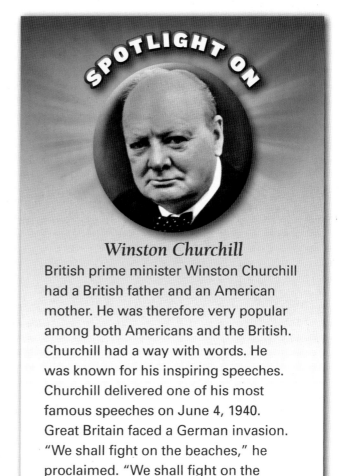

SPOTLIGHT ON

Winston Churchill

British prime minister Winston Churchill had a British father and an American mother. He was therefore very popular among both Americans and the British. Churchill had a way with words. He was known for his inspiring speeches. Churchill delivered one of his most famous speeches on June 4, 1940. Great Britain faced a German invasion. "We shall fight on the beaches," he proclaimed. "We shall fight on the landing grounds, we shall fight in the fields and in the streets, we shall fight in the hills; we shall never surrender."

The air raid lasted about 90 minutes. Pearl Harbor was in smoking ruins. Four U.S. battleships were sunk. Many more vessels were damaged, and 2,402 men were killed. It was one of the worst military defeats in U.S. history.

The USS *Arizona* was among the U.S. ships sunk during the Pearl Harbor attack.

A War Across Two Oceans

The Pearl Harbor attack was a desperate Japanese gamble. Japan had few natural resources. Japanese leaders believed they had to expand to obtain the

A FIRSTHAND LOOK AT
THE USS *ARIZONA* MEMORIAL

At the start of the Pearl Harbor attack, a Japanese bomb tore through the deck of the battleship USS *Arizona* and exploded. The *Arizona* sank within minutes. More than 1,000 sailors lost their lives. In 1962, the USS *Arizona* Memorial was built above the sunken ship. See page 60 for a link to find out how you can visit the memorial.

materials they needed. But the United States, with its powerful Pacific fleet based in Hawaii, stood in the way of such expansion. Japan hoped its attack would leave U.S. leaders stunned and willing to negotiate. The plan backfired. The attack on Pearl Harbor only angered the United States. For the rest of the war, "Remember Pearl Harbor!" rang out as a U.S. battle cry.

Congress declared war on Japan the day after the Pearl Harbor attack. Germany and Italy declared war on the United States three days later. U.S. forces now had to fight in two **theaters of operation**: the European Theater and the Pacific Theater.

YESTERDAY'S HEADLINES

The attack on Pearl Harbor inspired strong feelings of patriotism throughout the United States. Many popular songs were written about the event. Some were sad songs about the attack itself. Others were upbeat songs about how the United States would defeat its enemies in battle. One of the biggest hits was Sammy Kaye's (above) "Remember Pearl Harbor." The song was heard on radios across the country and remained popular throughout the war. Its lyrics recall past U.S. victories and look toward a U.S. victory in World War II.

Let's remember Pearl Harbor
As we go to meet the foe.
Let's remember Pearl Harbor
As we did the Alamo.

CHAPTER 2

THE EUROPEAN THEATER

Winston Churchill (left) and Franklin Roosevelt (center) provided strong leadership for their countries during the war.

PRESIDENT FRANKLIN ROOSEVELT

had his first wartime conference with Prime Minister Winston Churchill in December 1941. At that conference, the two leaders adopted a "Europe first" policy. They determined that Germany was their greatest threat. Hitler's leadership had to end as soon as possible. The Allies (primarily Great Britain, the United States, and the Soviet Union) agreed to concentrate their efforts on defeating Germany first. They would then move on to Italy and Japan.

Dwight Eisenhower (seated) commanded forces against German general Erwin Rommel in North Africa.

North Africa

U.S. troops under the command of General Dwight D. Eisenhower landed in North Africa in November 1942. For almost two years, the British had waged a battle with the Germans and Italians in the North African deserts. Battle lines shifted constantly as British soldiers drove the Axis forces back, only to see them rally and retake the offensive. The flat desert was perfect tank country. The Germans were led by General Erwin Rommel. Rommel was a superb tank commander.

In February 1943, U.S. soldiers faced Rommel at Kasserine Pass in North Africa. In this first major action, the Americans proved to be no match for the experienced German fighters. They were forced to retreat. They suffered thousands of casualties. More men and equipment were brought to the **fronts**. The Allies finally drove Rommel out of North Africa in May 1943. About 250,000 Axis soldiers surrendered to the Americans and the British.

A VIEW FROM ABROAD

Not all Germans believed that Hitler was a good leader. Rommel had supporters who believed that he would make a better leader than Hitler. Rommel did not disagree with them. The supporters began plotting to kill Hitler without telling Rommel. Rommel did not believe murder should be used for political gain. The plot was discovered, and Hitler escaped death.

Hitler did not tolerate such rebellion. Even though Rommel was not involved in the plot, he was included in Hitler's revenge. Hitler gave him the option of either swallowing a poison pill and dying an honorable death, or going through a trial where his reputation would be destroyed. Rommel chose the poison. He died on October 14, 1944.

The Mediterranean

Winston Churchill urged the Allies to invade the European countries controlled by Hitler through the Mediterranean Sea by landing on the island of Sicily and mainland Italy. He believed that this would be the best route to victory. Churchill referred to the Mediterranean region as the "soft underbelly" of Europe.

U.S. and British forces landed on the beaches of Sicily in July 1943. The Allies secured the island after 39 days of fighting. Benito Mussolini fell from power during the invasion. A new Italian government sought peace with the Allies. Adolf Hitler sent a large army into Italy. The Italians found themselves occupied by their former allies.

U.S. and British forces moved north into Italy from the beaches of Sicily.

Benito Mussolini's (left) alliance with Germany led to Italy's invasion by the Nazis.

Mussolini and his girlfriend were captured by members of the Italian resistance in April 1945. They were both shot to death. Their bodies were hung upside down in the Italian city of Milan. Angry citizens pelted them with rocks and sticks.

The Allies launched a two-pronged invasion of Italy in September 1943. The British landed near the tip of Calabria, located on the toe of Italy's "boot." U.S. forces landed far to the north at the city of Salerno. Southern Italy fell quickly to the Allies. Grinding combat developed to the north as the Germans established a

Allied forces captured Rome in June 1944.

defensive position in rugged mountain country. The
Allies tried to **flank** the Germans by landing behind their
lines at the city of Anzio. But the plan was ineffective.
The Germans continued to hold their ground. The Allies
marched into the Italian capital of Rome in June 1944.
The German infantry simply moved a few miles north
of Rome. The Mediterranean proved to be anything but
"the soft underbelly" of Europe that Winston Churchill
imagined it to be.

The Air War

Allied bombers operated from airfields in England and North Africa to attack targets in Europe. The British preferred night air raids because darkness made it more difficult for German fighter planes to locate them. The Americans believed daylight raids were more accurate. Between the two air forces, Germany was subject to round-the-clock bombing.

Allied leaders targeted German industries. But their bombs often fell on residential neighborhoods. The city of Hamburg was bombed in July 1943. The raid created an enormous ball of fire that sucked in air so fast that wind bursts toppled trees and overturned cars. Hamburg's chief of police called it "a fire typhoon such as was never

Hamburg, Germany, suffered heavy damage in the bombings of July 1943.

The U.S. Air Force used large bomber planes in the attack on Dresden.

before witnessed." The German city of Dresden had few industries. Many German families moved there because they thought it would be safe from air raids. Yet 1,300 Allied bombers struck Dresden in early 1945. About 25,000 civilians were killed.

A FIRSTHAND LOOK AT
D-DAY PHOTOS

The Allied troops landing on the beaches of Normandy has become one of the most well-known images of World War II. It has been portrayed in many popular movies, books, and even video games. But none of them can capture what the event was truly like. See page 60 for a link to view photos of D-Day online.

Victory in Europe

On June 6, 1944, a huge formation of transport planes roared over the English Channel toward the Normandy region of France. Inside were paratroopers who jumped into the darkness to begin the assault on Nazi-occupied Europe. Four thousand ships of various sizes bobbed in the waves offshore. They carried around 150,000 soldiers. It was D-Day, one of the largest combined air, sea, and land operations ever attempted.

The Allies got out of Normandy after six weeks of bitter combat and began a race across France. They liberated Paris on August 25, 1944. To the east, the Soviets marched ever closer to Germany. The Germans were now fighting a desperate war on two fronts. They seemed doomed.

Large numbers of Allied troops landed on the beaches of Normandy on D-Day.

Travel on foot was often difficult in the snowy Ardennes Forest of France.

Hitler had a final surprise for the Allies. In December 1944, a deafening German **artillery** attack rattled U.S. lines in the Ardennes Forest of France. Germany launched an attack with more than 200,000 soldiers supported by tanks. Allied leaders were stunned. No one believed the Germans had enough troops remaining to make such a powerful assault.

The German offensive during the winter of 1944 and 1945 was called the Battle of the Bulge. It was so named because the Germans' initial attack caused the Allied front lines to appear to "bulge" on maps. For the United States, it was the largest battle of World War II. Allied officers were surprised by the sudden enemy offensive. But Germany was the ultimate loser. The battle cost the Germans 100,000 casualties.

On April 30, 1945, Russian infantry units neared the German capital of Berlin, and the last battle of the European war broke out. Adolf Hitler sat in his underground bunker in the heart of the capital during the fighting. Hitler and his wife committed suicide when Russian troops were just blocks away. Germany officially surrendered to the Allies on May 7.

May 8, 1945, was V-E Day, Victory in Europe. Celebrations for V-E Day were brief and subdued. Everyone knew that Japan was still very much in the war.

TODAY'S PERSPECTIVE

As the Allies marched into Germany, they discovered **concentration camps**. Only then was Hitler's true evil revealed. In these camps, people were tortured and put to death in horrifying ways. Victims included Jews, Roma (Gypsies), the mentally and physically disabled, and any other group deemed "undesirable" by Nazi leaders. This great tragedy is known as the Holocaust. About six million Jews were killed during the Holocaust. Most people outside of Germany were unaware of these activities during the war. But we now understand the true horror of Nazi Germany.

CHAPTER 3

THE HOME FRONT

Many U.S. citizens kept gardens for growing vegetables and fruits during the war to increase the country's overall food supply.

MOST WARS CAUSE A GREAT deal of controversy. Many people do not want their countries to participate, and protests are common. But that was not the case during World War II in the United States. There were few negative views of the war. Hitler was seen as a power-hungry villain. Pearl Harbor had turned the Japanese into hated enemies. Most Americans saw the Axis as an evil force that needed to be destroyed for the good of humanity. Many Americans volunteered to fight in the war. And even those at home worked toward victory.

People were only allowed certain amounts of many food items during the war to make sure there was enough for everyone. Rations were tracked in booklets.

Living in Fear

American civilians fought their own war on a battleground known as the home front. The home front years were a time of hard work, sacrifice, and worries. Almost everyone had a friend or a relative in the military. They feared for the safety of their loved ones. Still, an exciting spirit gripped the nation. Never before or since had the country been so swept up in a single mission.

Every city held air raid drills. Neither the Japanese nor the Germans had airplanes that could reach American shores. But even farm towns in the middle of the country held these drills. Air raid drills also included blackouts, which were held at night and called for households to turn out their lights. Anyone careless enough to leave a light burning received a knock on the door and a scolding from a stern-faced air raid warden.

Weeks after Pearl Harbor, a sudden thunderstorm struck Los Angeles, California. Residents looked out their windows. Hundreds of men and women swore they saw Japanese bombers crossing the sky. There was no air raid on Los Angeles that night. No American city was

Students hid beneath their desks during air raid drills.

ever bombed during World War II. The imagined air raid on Los Angeles was the result of what was commonly called "war nerves."

Fear moved the nation into passing the Japanese **internment** law. The law was one of the most shameful measures ever taken in modern American history. Rumors circulated early in the war that Japanese Americans were secretly working with the Japanese military. These rumors were false. There was no evidence pointing to disloyalty among the Japanese American citizens of the United States.

Trains full of Japanese Americans were sent to the internment camps.

President Roosevelt signed Executive Order 9066 in February 1942. The order removed all Japanese Americans from the West Coast and sent them to internment camps farther inland. The law affected some 100,000 Japanese Americans. Many lost their homes and their businesses when they were required to move.

The War of Machines

The United States had the most advanced economy in the world. The country had suffered through the Great Depression in the 1930s. Many factories had fallen silent during this time. Those factories sprang back to life in wartime. Plants that once made typewriters now manufactured machine guns. Car producers assembled military jeeps and trucks.

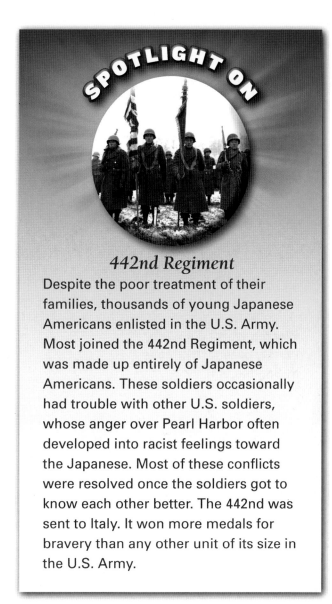

SPOTLIGHT ON

442nd Regiment

Despite the poor treatment of their families, thousands of young Japanese Americans enlisted in the U.S. Army. Most joined the 442nd Regiment, which was made up entirely of Japanese Americans. These soldiers occasionally had trouble with other U.S. soldiers, whose anger over Pearl Harbor often developed into racist feelings toward the Japanese. Most of these conflicts were resolved once the soldiers got to know each other better. The 442nd was sent to Italy. It won more medals for bravery than any other unit of its size in the U.S. Army.

Many American women had a major change in their lifestyles during the war. Before the war, three out of four American women were housewives. They stayed at home to cook, clean, and tend to children. Now the women were desperately needed in factories. Women soon outnumbered men in many **industrial** plants. The American workforce was 36 percent female by 1945.

V Is for Victory

Letters to servicemen were known as victory mail. The posters that hung in factories and urged people to work hard were called victory posters.

Women worked a wide variety of industrial jobs during the war.

Children around the country helped to collect large amounts of scrap metal to be used for war materials.

Even children were expected to work for victory. Boy Scouts and Campfire Girls participated in scrap drives. The scrap drives were massive recycling efforts. Kids picked up scrap items in alleys and gave them to recycling companies. The items were recycled into supplies for the military.

A FIRSTHAND LOOK AT
ROSIE THE RIVETER

Rosie the Riveter was a hero of the home front. The character was a muscular but pretty young lady on wartime posters who confidently told the country, "We can do it!" See page 60 for a link to see a Rosie the Riveter poster online.

Legendary actor John Wayne starred in *Back to Bataan*.

Small vegetable plots tended by families sprouted in every city and town. They were called victory gardens. Planting a victory garden was considered a patriotic duty. Such gardens allowed the government to send farm-raised food overseas. By 1944, some 20 million victory gardens produced almost one-third of the nation's vegetables.

Movies were the nation's most popular form of entertainment during the war. The film *Wake Island* (1942) told of a bitter U.S. defeat at the hands of the Japanese. Later in the war, the film *Back to Bataan* (1945) showed the U.S. Army fighting the Japanese in the Philippines. Even children's cartoons had a wartime bent. In one 1944 cartoon, Bugs Bunny gives hand grenades disguised as ice cream bars to Japanese soldiers.

Wartime songs paid tribute to heroes in uniform. "Comin' in on a Wing and a Prayer" told of a bomber crew trying to fly its damaged aircraft to its home field. "Bell Bottom Trousers" celebrated young sailors.

An unexpected disaster struck the United States on April 12, 1945. President Franklin Roosevelt collapsed and died just moments after saying that he had "a terrific headache." Roosevelt was 63 years old. Close associates knew the pressures of the war were taking a toll on Roosevelt. But his declining health had been kept secret from the public. Americans were shocked and saddened by the loss of their leader. Vice President Harry Truman took office immediately. The "V for Victory" spirit of the home front continued.

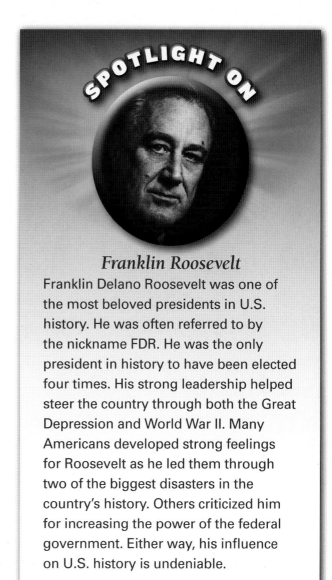

SPOTLIGHT ON

Franklin Roosevelt

Franklin Delano Roosevelt was one of the most beloved presidents in U.S. history. He was often referred to by the nickname FDR. He was the only president in history to have been elected four times. His strong leadership helped steer the country through both the Great Depression and World War II. Many Americans developed strong feelings for Roosevelt as he led them through two of the biggest disasters in the country's history. Others criticized him for increasing the power of the federal government. Either way, his influence on U.S. history is undeniable.

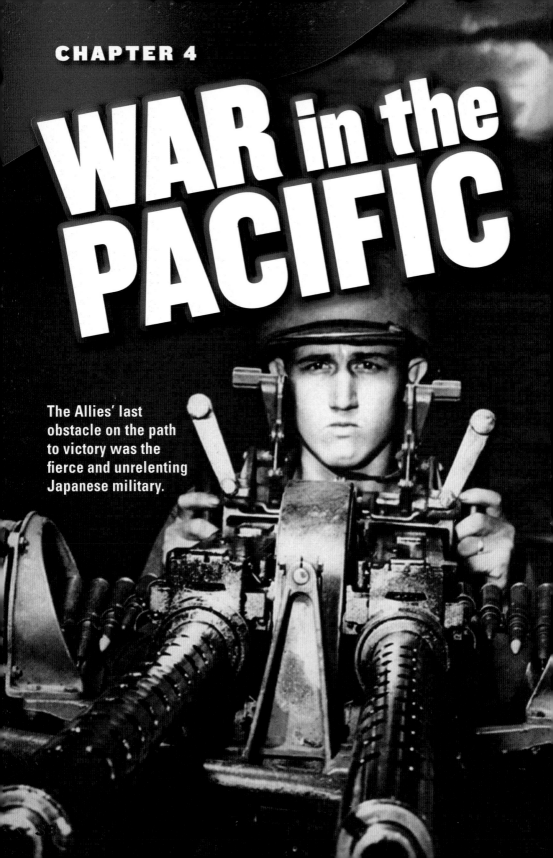

CHAPTER 4

WAR in the PACIFIC

The Allies' last obstacle on the path to victory was the fierce and unrelenting Japanese military.

To THE AMERICANS, THE
Japanese seemed to be a worse enemy than the
Germans. The Japanese shot Americans who
tried to surrender and tortured prisoners. U.S.
forces were just as brutal in their treatment of the
Japanese. They had not forgotten the attack on
Pearl Harbor. U.S. soldiers captured few Japanese
prisoners. The war in the Pacific took on a
particularly vile nature.

U.S. forces had no choice but to surrender to the Japanese in April 1942 at Bataan.

The Rising Sun

Weeks after their victory at Pearl Harbor, Japanese soldiers conquered British territory on Malaya and in the Dutch colonies of the East Indies. Japanese diplomats claimed they were freeing Asian people from European control. But they actually enslaved the conquered people and treated them far worse than the Europeans had.

In April 1942, a U.S.-led army surrendered to the Japanese on the Bataan Peninsula in the Philippines. General Douglas MacArthur, the American commander, escaped the Philippines. MacArthur issued a promise soon after he left: "I shall return."

Japan enjoyed conquest after conquest in the first four months of the war. Its flag, the Rising Sun, flew above a Pacific empire that spread over 1 million square miles (2.6 million square kilometers).

The Battle of Midway

In May 1942, the U.S. naval base on Midway Island sent out a radio message saying that it was running low on water. The message was not broadcast in code, as most messages from the naval base were. Code would have prevented the Japanese from knowing what the Americans were saying. But this message was also a lie. The base had plenty of water.

U.S. intelligence teams had been intercepting Japanese radio signals for months. They had cracked the

YESTERDAY'S HEADLINES

Around 100,000 U.S. and Filipino soldiers were taken prisoner at Bataan. This began a horrific chapter in the war known as the Bataan Death March. The men were marched 65 miles (105 km) in the brutal Philippine heat to prison camps. They were purposely denied water and food. When men fell from exhaustion, Japanese guards shot them and left the bodies to rot. About 7,000 Americans and Filipinos died on the march. Word of this cruel treatment leaked out to U.S. military units and to the public. This caused the hatred of the Japanese enemy to grow stronger.

Japanese military code bit by bit. The teams knew that the Japanese planned to invade an American base called, in code language, AF. Intelligence officers suspected AF was Midway Island. Shortly after the Americans sent their false message, they intercepted another Japanese code transmission. This one said AF was running out of water. Now the Americans knew for certain that AF was Midway Island.

The Battle of Midway took place in June 1942. The first Japanese strike came not at Midway but hundreds of miles to the north where carrier-based aircraft bombed the Aleutian Islands. This attack was a **feint**. Japanese officers

U.S. bombers caught the Japanese by surprise during the Battle of Midway.

hoped to draw the American fleet north. This would clear the way for their main assault on Midway Island. But the Americans knew better than to take the bait. They kept three aircraft carriers in the waters off Midway. On the morning of June 4, some 100 Japanese aircraft took off from four carriers and hit airfields on Midway. They did not know that three enemy carriers were sailing nearby. Suddenly, U.S. bombers roared toward the Japanese fleet. American bombs rained down on the carriers' decks. Three Japanese carriers were destroyed in a matter of minutes. U.S. forces sank a fourth Japanese carrier the next day.

The battle was a major turning point in the Pacific war. The Japanese navy lost four carriers to the U.S. Navy's one. Some 300 Japanese planes were destroyed. Many of Japan's finest pilots were killed. Never again was the proud Japanese navy able to take the offensive in the Pacific.

Island-Hopping

The U.S. military took an island-by-island strategy to approach the shores of Japan. They skipped over the less important islands and conquered the others one by one. This strategy came to be called "island-hopping."

Marines and soldiers splashed ashore on the jungle-covered island of Guadalcanal in August 1942. They experienced their first "banzai charge" on this island. Japanese officers sent waves of men running toward the Americans while shouting "banzai!" Loosely translated, the word means "may our emperor live 10,000 years." The

U.S. troops stormed the beaches of Guadalcanal.

banzai charges were fearsome to witness. But they actually played into U.S. strength. The U.S. troops always carried plenty of artillery and machine guns with them into battle. The wild charges brought Japanese soldiers into the open and made them easier to kill. The battle at Guadalcanal lasted six months. The Japanese lost 25,000 men.

A huge American fleet ringed the tiny Pacific island of Tarawa in November 1943. The enormous guns of battleships and cruisers pounded the island. From the decks of ships, U.S. Marines who were trained in **amphibious** warfare watched the attack in awe. Surely no one could live through this rain of explosives. The marines soon discovered that Tarawa held thousands of

Japanese soldiers. All of them were determined to fight till death. The Battle for Tarawa concluded after 76 hours. More than 3,000 U.S. troops were killed or wounded.

Many navy leaders wanted to bypass the entire Philippine Island group. But General MacArthur argued that the Philippines must be liberated from Japanese rule. The Filipino people had been fighting a brave war for many months. To bypass the island group would be thought of as an act of betrayal. President Roosevelt agreed and authorized an invasion of the Philippines. The general could now keep his promise to return.

With Douglas MacArthur in command, U.S. soldiers landed on the Philippines in October 1944. U.S. forces occupied the Philippine capital of Manila after four months of tough fighting. The Pacific war's last major sea battle was fought during the Philippine operation. The

General MacArthur (fourth from right) led the U.S. invasion of the Philippines.

Japanese used their remaining ships to attack the U.S. fleet at Leyte Gulf. The Japanese lost several battleships and aircraft carriers. Leyte was the final death blow for the once mighty Japanese navy.

Iwo Jima and Okinawa

Iwo Jima is an ugly, treeless volcanic island. But it held an airfield needed by the Americans. Some 60,000 marines landed there in February 1945. The Battle of Iwo Jima was savage from the opening moments. No longer did the Japanese launch wild banzai charges. Instead, Japanese officers ordered their men to stay in fortified positions and force the Americans to come to them. Six thousand marines were killed and 25,000 were wounded in the 36-day battle. About 20,000 Japanese

The U.S. forces bombarded the Japanese defenders with large shells in the attack on Iwo Jima.

Kamikaze pilots sacrificed their lives to defend against the U.S. attackers.

defenders died on the island. Only 216 Japanese soldiers were taken alive. Those captives were either wounded or too dazed by artillery blasts to continue the fight.

American forces invaded the island of Okinawa on April 1, 1945. A fleet of American ships supported the invasion. From out of the sky came Japanese aircraft piloted by men determined to kill Americans and kill themselves in the process. They were the kamikazes. Kamikazes were the latest Japanese weapon. They flew their planes directly at U.S. ships and crashed on their decks. U.S. sailors were both horrified and amazed at their enemy's dedication to death. Thirty-four U.S. ships were sunk and 368 were damaged in the waters off Okinawa. More than 12,000

A FIRSTHAND LOOK AT
THE RAISING OF THE FLAG ON IWO JIMA

Three days after the landing on Iwo Jima, a platoon of marines fought its way to the top of Mount Suribachi, the island's highest point. The men raised the American flag at the peak. Men on the ground cheered, and ships at sea blew their horns. It was determined that the first flag was too small. So the Marines raised a second flag. This second flag raising was photographed by newspaper cameraman Joe Rosenthal. See page 60 for a link to see the photo and learn more about this historic moment.

American sailors lost their lives. Constant combat and intense fear drove many men insane. Others suffered from nightmares for the rest of their lives.

The land battle in southern Okinawa was one of the bloodiest of the war. So many bodies covered the ground that the men could not bury them fast enough. The stink of decomposing flesh was overwhelming. Rains began to fall in May, adding to the misery.

Rain of Ruin

A powerful new American bomber took to the skies over the Pacific in late 1944. The B-29 was the largest combat aircraft of the war. The silvery four-engine plane flew at 350 miles per hour (563 kph) and carried 20,000 pounds (9,072 kilograms) of bombs. American generals believed that the new bomber was a war-winning machine. But the B-29 operated from high **altitudes**. Its bombing runs were inaccurate.

General Curtis E. LeMay took command of B-29 operations and ordered the firebombing of Japanese cities. The general believed that if whole cities were set on fire, the flames would spread to factories and shipbuilding facilities. A formation of 325 bombers hit the Japanese capital of Tokyo on the night of March 10, 1945. French newspaper reporter Robert Guillain lived in Tokyo at the time. He wrote that bombs "were raining down by the thousands . . . spreading a wash of dancing flames."

Japan was being bombed regularly by the summer of 1945. Its once mighty fleet had been sunk. But Japanese leaders refused to talk peace. The Americans had no choice but to plan an invasion of Japan. Everyone knew how furiously Japanese soldiers defended islands such as Iwo Jima and Okinawa. The thought of a landing on Japan itself made U.S. soldiers shudder.

Firebombs destroyed huge portions of Tokyo.

On August 5, 1945, a lone B-29 took off from Tinian Island. It carried an atomic bomb. The atomic bomb was the most destructive weapon ever built. The development of this bomb was so secret that only a few dozen Americans knew of its existence. The B-29 dropped the first atomic bomb on Hiroshima, Japan, the morning of August 6. The city disappeared in a great ball of fire. People directly below the blast were burned in the time it takes to blink an eye. Perhaps as many as 90,000 Hiroshima residents died on the first day. Deaths continued because **radiation** released by the bomb caused damage that could kill people months or even years later.

Events moved rapidly after the Hiroshima bombing. On August 7, President Harry S. Truman demanded the Japanese accept surrender terms. "If they do not now ac-

Very few buildings were left standing in Hiroshima after the atomic bomb was dropped.

cept our terms they may expect a rain of ruin from the air, the like of which has never been seen on this earth," he said. The Japanese refused to surrender, and the U.S. dropped another atomic bomb on August 9. This one was aimed at the city of Nagasaki. The Japanese government finally announced on August 14 that it would surrender to the United States.

People cheered into the night. Strangers hugged and kissed each other. But an unsettling feeling dampened the celebrations. The newly invented atomic bomb was a weapon that could destroy the world. The end of the war brought humankind into the very frightening atomic age.

TODAY'S PERSPECTIVE

Sadako Sasaki was two years old when the atomic bomb exploded about a mile from her Hiroshima home. At first, it appeared she was unhurt. But Sadako became sick with leukemia, a cancer of the blood, when she was in sixth grade. Leukemia is one of the many diseases associated with atomic radiation. An old Japanese saying holds that if a sick person makes a thousand paper cranes he or she will become well. Sadako started this project but died after completing 964 cranes. Her schoolmates made the remaining cranes and buried them with her. Today a statue of Sadako stands at the Hiroshima Children's Peace Monument. She is holding the figure of a paper crane. Beneath the statue are carved the words, "This is our cry, this is our prayer: peace in the world."

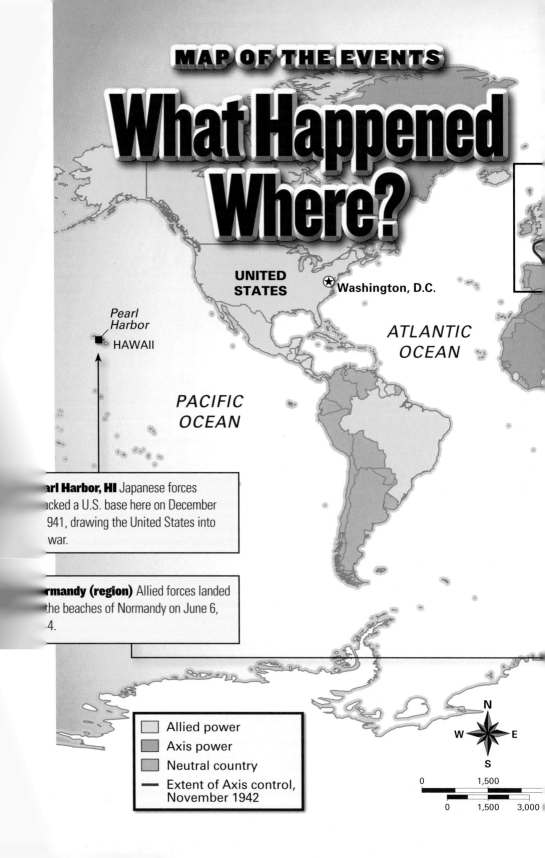

MAP OF THE EVENTS

What Happened Where?

UNITED STATES

⊛ Washington, D.C.

Pearl Harbor

◼ HAWAII

ATLANTIC OCEAN

PACIFIC OCEAN

arl Harbor, HI Japanese forces
acked a U.S. base here on December
941, drawing the United States into
war.

rmandy (region) Allied forces landed
the beaches of Normandy on June 6,
4.

☐ Allied power

◼ Axis power

◼ Neutral country

— Extent of Axis control,
November 1942

N
W ✦ E
S

0   1,500
0   1,500   3,000

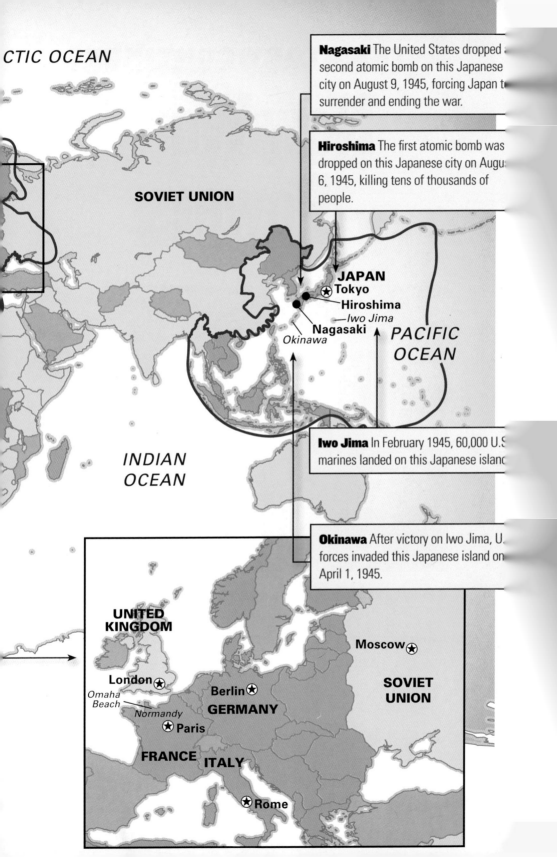

CTIC OCEAN

Nagasaki The United States dropped a second atomic bomb on this Japanese city on August 9, 1945, forcing Japan to surrender and ending the war.

Hiroshima The first atomic bomb was dropped on this Japanese city on August 6, 1945, killing tens of thousands of people.

SOVIET UNION

JAPAN
⭐Tokyo
Hiroshima
Iwo Jima
Nagasaki
Okinawa

PACIFIC OCEAN

INDIAN OCEAN

Iwo Jima In February 1945, 60,000 U.S. marines landed on this Japanese island

Okinawa After victory on Iwo Jima, U.S. forces invaded this Japanese island on April 1, 1945.

UNITED KINGDOM

Moscow⭐

London⭐
Omaha Beach
Normandy
Berlin⭐
GERMANY

SOVIET UNION

⭐Paris

FRANCE ITALY

⭐Rome

New World Powers

U.S. forces occupied Japan after the war ended.

Enemies in war quickly became friends in peace. Japan was occupied by American soldiers. Most of the soldiers had hated the Japanese when they fought them in the Pacific Campaign. But they soon learned to admire the Japanese people they met. Some American men fell in love with Japanese women, married them, and stayed in Japan. U.S. soldiers also lived among their one-time enemies in Germany. Old hatreds eventually faded away.

The end of World War II left the Soviet Union and the United States as the two dominant world powers. A new conflict called the Cold War developed. The Cold War was not based on combat. It was an intense rivalry between the United States and the Soviet Union. Each nation had a different type of government and hoped to show its superiority over the other. Both sides had powerful atomic weapons. This meant that the world could see destruction like it had never seen before, if the rivalry turned violent. Cold War tensions continued well into the 1980s before the two countries agreed to resolve their differences.

The Berlin Wall separated Soviet-controlled East Berlin from U.S.-controlled West Berlin in Germany during the Cold War.

28 YEARS, FROM 1961 TO 1989.

INFLUENTIAL INDIVIDUALS

Winston Churchill

Franklin D. Roosevelt

Winston Churchill (1874–1965) was the British prime minister who led his nation through the most difficult periods of World War II. He was a popular figure in the United States, and his mother was American.

Douglas MacArthur (1880–1964) grew up in an army family. He attended the military academy at West Point, where he graduated first in his class in 1903. He was a brave officer and had a brilliant military mind. Critics claimed that perhaps he was too brilliant. He regularly ignored orders from superiors, including orders issued by the president of the United States, and he set his own policies.

Franklin D. Roosevelt (1882–1945) was born to a wealthy and politically powerful New York family. He was elected president four times and held the office longer than any other president. He guided the country through both the Great Depression and World War II.

Benito Mussolini (1883–1945) was the leader of Italy for 21 years. An ally of Adolf Hitler, he dreamed of restoring Italy to the power it enjoyed in the Roman era. Instead, Italy fell under the power of the German army.

Harry S. Truman (1884–1972) was a little-known senator from Missouri when Roosevelt picked him to run for vice president in 1944. He had served as vice president for only 82 days when Roosevelt died, thrusting Truman into the presidency. He led the country through the end of the war and the postwar settlements.

Adolf Hitler

Adolf Hitler (1889–1945) was the dictator of Germany. He is thought of as one of the most evil men in history. A veteran of World War I, he rose to power by jailing or assassinating his opponents. He gave impassioned speeches and inspired his followers.

Dwight D. Eisenhower (1890–1969) was a little-known army colonel before the war. As the war progressed, he rose to become the most powerful general in the European theater. Always admired by the public, he was elected U.S. president for two terms (1953–1961).

TIMELINE

1918	1931	1933	1937
November World War I ends in defeat for Germany.	Japan invades Chinese territory.	Adolf Hitler rises to become the dictator of Germany.	An undeclared war between Japan and China begins.

1942	1943

April 9 The U.S.-led army in the Philippines surrenders to the Japanese.

June 4–5 The United States sinks four Japanese aircraft carriers at the Battle of Midway, dealing a crippling blow to the Japanese navy.

August 7 U.S. Marines land at Guadalcanal to begin offensive warfare in the Pacific.

November 7–8 American troops under General Dwight D. Eisenhower land in North Africa.

July 10 The Allies invade Sicily.

September 3 The Allies invade Italy.

November 20 U.S. Marines land at the Pacific island of Tarawa.

1939

September 1 Germany invades Poland, beginning World War II.

September 3 Britain and France declare war on Germany.

1940

June 22 France surrenders to Germany.

July Germany begins an intense air war against Great Britain.

1941

June 22 Germany invades Russia.

December 7 Japan bombs the U.S. naval base at Pearl Harbor.

December 8 The United States declares war on Japan.

December 11 Germany and Italy declare war on the United States.

1944

June 5 U.S. forces enter Rome.

June 6 The Allies land in France on D-Day.

August 25 Paris is liberated by the Allies.

October 20 U.S. forces invade the Philippines.

December 16 The Battle of the Bulge begins.

1945

April 12 President Franklin Roosevelt dies suddenly.

April 30 Adolf Hitler commits suicide.

May 7 Germany surrenders to the Allies.

August 6 A B-29 drops an atomic bomb on Hiroshima, Japan.

August 9 A B-29 drops an atomic bomb on Nagasaki, Japan.

August 14 Japan agrees to surrender.

LIVING HISTORY

Primary sources provide firsthand evidence about a topic. Witnesses to a historical event create primary sources. They include autobiographies, newspaper reports of the time, oral histories, photographs, and memoirs. A secondary source analyzes primary sources, and is one step or more removed from the event. Secondary sources include textbooks, encyclopedias, and commentaries.

D-Day Photos D-Day is one of the most memorable and visually striking events of World War II. To see a wide range of photos from the event and the hours leading up to it, visit *www.life.com /gallery/24691/image/50372111#index/0*

The Raising of the Flag on Iwo Jima Joe Rosenthal's photograph of U.S. soldiers raising the American flag on Iwo Jima is one of the most well-known photographs in U.S. history. Rosenthal won a Pulitzer Prize for the photograph. To see the photo and find out more about its history, visit *www.loc.gov/exhibits/treasures /trm023.html*

Rosie the Riveter Rosie the Riveter was an inspirational symbol for the millions of American women who took jobs in factories during the war. To see a Rosie the Riveter poster and photos of women at work during World War II, visit *www.fhwa.dot.gov/wit/rosie.htm*

The USS *Arizona* Memorial Thousands of U.S. sailors died in the attack on Pearl Harbor. A memorial was constructed above the sunken ruins of the USS *Arizona*. Today, the memorial is part of the Valor in the Pacific National Monument in Hawaii. To find out how you can visit the monument and to learn more about its history, visit *www.nps.gov/valr/index.htm*

RESOURCES

Books

Hama, Larry. *The Battle of Guadalcanal: Land and Sea Warfare in the South Pacific*. New York: Rosen Publishing, 2007.

Hama, Larry. *The Battle of Iwo Jima: Guerilla Warfare in the Pacific*. New York: Rosen Publishing, 2007.

Huey, Lois Miner. *Voices of World War II: Stories from the Front Lines*. Mankato, MN: Capstone Press, 2011.

Murray, Doug. *D-Day: The Liberation of Europe Begins*. New York: Rosen Central, 2008.

Perritano, John. *World War II*. New York: Franklin Watts, 2010.

Stein, R. Conrad. *World War II in Europe: From Normandy to Berlin*. Berkeley Heights, NJ: Enslow Publishers, 2011.

Wagner, Melissa, and Dan Bryant. *The Big Book of World War II*. Philadelphia: RP Classics, 2009.

Web Sites

History.com—World War II
www.history.com/topics/world-war-ii
Check out videos, photos, and articles about World War II from the History Channel.

National Archives—Pictures of World War II
www.archives.gov/research/military/ww2/photos/
Search through a large collection of World War II photographs from the U.S. National Archives.

Visit this Scholastic Web site for more information on World War II:
www.factsfornow.scholastic.com

GLOSSARY

altitudes (AL-ti-toodz) the heights of things above the ground or above sea level

amphibious (am-FIB-ee-uhs) effective on both land and water

artillery (ahr-TIL-uh-ree) large weapons that are fired from a distance

blitzkrieg (BLITS-kreeg) fast, powerful style of warfare used by Germany during World War II

casualties (KAZH-oo-uhl-teez) people killed or wounded during warfare

concentration camps (kahn-suhn-TRAY-shuhn KAMPS) Nazi camps where Jews and other minorities were tortured and killed in large numbers

dictator (DIK-tay-tur) a ruler who has complete control of a country, often by force

feint (FAYNT) a blow or movement meant to take attention away from the real point of attack

flank (FLANGK) to be at the side of something or someone

fronts (FRUHNTS) the areas where armies meet and fight

industrial (in-DUH-stree-uhl) having to do with manufacturing companies and other businesses

infantry (IN-fuhn-tree) soldiers who fight on foot

internment (in-TURN-muhnt) confinement

radiation (ray-dee-AY-shuhn) atomic particles that are sent out from a radioactive substance

theaters of operation (THEE-uh-turz OV ah-puh-RAY-shuhn) specific parts of the world where a war is fought

INDEX

Page numbers in *italics* indicate illustrations.

ABOUT THE AUTHOR

R. Conrad Stein was born in Chicago. At age 18, he enlisted in the U.S. Marine Corps and served three years. After his discharge from the Marines, he attended the University of Illinois where he graduated with a degree in history. Today, Mr. Stein is a full-time author. Over the years, he has published more than 200 books, most of them history books for young readers. He now lives in Chicago with his wife, Deborah Kent, who is also an author of books for young readers, and their daughter, Janna.